GETTING  IT RIGHT

Safe
Slo-Cooker
Recipes

GETTING IT RIGHT

Safe Slo-Cooker Recipes

Annette Yates

foulsham
LONDON • NEW YORK • TORONTO • SYDNEY

foulsham
Yeovil Road, Slough, Berkshire, SL1 4JH

These Recipes represent a small selection from:
Tower Slo-Cookbook

ISBN 0-572-01921-1

Printed in Great Britain at St. Edmundsbury Press, Bury St. Edmunds.

Rating

Throughout the book the recipes have been given
a rating.

    means the recipe is easy to prepare

    means the recipe needs a little special care
during part or all of the preparation

    means the recipe is suitable for freezing

    means the heat settings and cooking times
given in these recipes must *not* be altered

    means recipes should *not* be prepared by the
one-step method.

INTRODUCING SLOW COOKING

Slow cooking is a time tested method of successful food preparation. The advent of electrical appliances specifically designed to cope with slow cooking simply adds an up-dated convenience to our busy lifestyles.

Just prepare the ingredients and place them in your Slo-Cooker before leaving home and return to a delicious hot meal. And meals are ready when you are; because of the time range there is little chance of them spoiling even if you are an hour or two late.

Your Slo-Cooker may be used day or night. Cook tomorrow's lunch or breakfast overnight, for example. Use the Slo-Cooker while you are at home, too, and appreciate the feeling of freedom knowing that the meal is cooking itself and the satisfaction that you are also economising on fuel.

The gently simmered (and often inexpensive) dishes that our grandparents prepared can be reproduced with great authenticity in your Slo-Cooker.

I hope you will enjoy the recipes in the pages to follow. Use them as a basis to experiment and develop your own favourite ideas to perfection. You will probably find, like I have, that the Slo-Cooker is best stored on the kitchen work surface where it is always handy for use. It looks very attractive, too. Use your other kitchen equipment to complement it and vice versa. You will find, for example, that some of the recipes will require the use of a blender for liquidising and pans for frying.

Finally, the majority of the recipes in this book are designed for all day cooking; but try those with shorter cooking times, or use the Slo-Cooker on High when you need a meal in a short time or for mid-day, when you have to go out for part of the day, when you want to get on with other chores around the house, or simply when you want a few hours to yourself.

Annette Yates

ABOUT THE RECIPES

The recipes in this book have been tested in the Tower range of Slo-Cookers. When using recipes in the following pages it is a good idea to compare the cooking time with a similar one in the manufacturer's recipe/instruction book. Some recipes have been developed to feed 6 or more persons but it is a simple matter to decrease or increase quantities to suit your requirements and the capacity of your slow cooker and cooking times will vary only slightly.

All recipes give instructions for pre-heating. Your manufacturer's instruction book will give details for your particular model. The methods of preparation in the recipes have been developed to produce the best results in terms of appearance, texture and flavour. This often includes browning of meat, light sautéeing of vegetables and thickening of liquids before slow cooking. If preparation has to be done early in the morning, before leaving for work, for example, you may prefer to omit any pre-heating of the food before slow cooking. Or, you can prepare the ingredients the evening before, refrigerate them, and place them in the Slo-Cooker next morning, without pre-frying. This is the One-Step method and cooking times will need to be extended, see the separate check-point list on page 14.

Your Slo-Cooker and your freezer

Your Slo-Cooker and your freezer can be the best of friends. It is a simple matter to prepare large quantities of food in the Slo-Cooker—some to eat immediately and some to freeze for a later date. See the notes about quantities on page 15.

More information about slow cooking and freezing is to be found in the introduction to each section and specific instructions for freezing individual recipes are given at the end of the method where appropriate. Frozen raw meat, poultry and fish must always be thawed thoroughly before slow cooking.

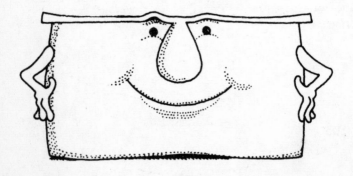

PREPARING YOUR FOOD

Vegetables take longer to cook than meat. They should therefore, be cut up into thin slices or diced ($\frac{1}{4}$ inch/$\frac{1}{2}$ cm.), placed near the bottom of the Slo-Cooker and immersed in the cooking liquid. If you are browning meat for the same recipe sauté the vegetables for a few minutes too.

Season sparingly; check again just before serving.

Completely thaw frozen vegetables and add them during the final hour of the cooking period.

Add milk and cream to savoury dishes during the final half hour since long cooking could cause them to separate.

If your Slo-Cooker is fitted with a removable pot, cooked dishes can be browned under the grill or covered with a topping and crisped in a pre-heated oven.

Add dumplings to soups or stews for the final $\frac{1}{2}$ hour and switch to the High setting for this time.

Use quick-cooking varieties of pasta or rice. Macaroni and lasagne should be softened in boiling water for a few minutes. When using raw rice extra liquid is needed ($\frac{1}{4}$ pt./150 ml./$\frac{2}{3}$ cup liquid for 4 oz./100 g./$\frac{3}{4}$ cup rice). No additional liquid required when cooked rice is used.

Add thickening agents at the start of slow cooking. Alternatively, mix the flour or cornflour with a little cold water and stir it into the ingredients for the final 1–1$\frac{1}{2}$ hours of cooking.

Dry cooking—such as Baked Potatoes—is not advisable since it could damage your Slo-Cooker.

When adapting recipes for slow cooking use about half the normal quantity of liquid since there is less evaporation. Make sure that root vegetables are covered.

Advantages of Slow Cooking

Your Slo-Cooker is superb for preparing soups, stocks, casseroles and stews. Flavours mix, blend and develop to produce concentrated, rich and tasty results. All the flavour is sealed in the pot. Economies are made in terms of fuel, money, effort and time. Fuel savings alone can be as much as 80% on normal cooking times. The efficient built-in insulation means only the food inside the Slo-Cooker heats up, not the whole kitchen.

Foods cooked in the Slo-Cooker remain attractively whole. This is a distinct advantage when cooking fruit, fish, etc. There is no need to turn or stir the food as it is not likely to overcook or boil over or stick and there are no hot spots to cause burning. The gentle heat results in less evaporation of liquids so there is little chance of food drying out. The steam condenses on the lid and returns to the pot. In doing so it forms a seal which retains heat and flavour. The gentle heat also tenderizes tough meat beautifully and joints of meat shrink less when cooked in the Slo-Cooker.

A Slo-Cooker is ideal for flexible meals. Once the cooking is completed the food can be kept safely on the Low setting for several hours without spoiling; part to be eaten immediately and part to be kept warm for latecomers. Convenience is a key factor, the Slo-Cooker is easy to use and can be operated day or night. Your evening meal can be placed in it and left all day to cook. On the other hand should you wish it to be ready for mid-day it can be cooked on High setting. A Slo-Cooker is ideal for any busy person and a boon to anyone who entertains.

Finally, slow cooking, with its gentle, moist action can be of great help when preparing food for special diets, particularly fat-free diets.

One-step Slo-Cooking

The one-step method of placing the cold ingredients in the Slo-Cooker and leaving them to cook all day, or all night, is suitable for those who can spend only a limited time on preparation.

Checkpoints for One-step Slo-Cooking

Always pre-heat the Slo-Cooker – check with your manufacturer's instruction book for the required time.

Mix the thickening agent (flour or cornflour) with a little cold water to form a paste and stir in with the ingredients. Alternatively, coat the meat with flour before adding to the Slo-Cooker. When the thickening agent is tomato purée or condensed soup, ensure these are mixed well with the other ingredients. Add the liquid which must be boiling.

When roasting brush the inside of the Slo-Cooker and the joint or bird with cooking oil.

Remember that root vegetables such as onions, potatoes, carrots etc, must be cut into small pieces ($\frac{1}{4}$ in./$\frac{1}{2}$ cm.). Those which tend to discolour, such as potatoes, should be covered with the cooking liquid to avoid browning during the heating-up period.

Always mix the ingredients well. This prevents foods (chopped bacon for instance) from sticking together. Stir soups and casseroles well before serving.

Do not leave ingredients in the Slo-Cooker overnight to be cooked the next day. If your Slo-Cooker has a removable pot, do not store the ingredients in the pot in a refrigerator before cooking.

When preparing recipes in this book by the one-step method add at least 3 hours on Low setting to the recommended cooking time. Recipes not suitable for one-step cooking are marked thus . .

How to use your Slo-Cooker

Follow manufacturers' instructions carefully when connecting the Slo-Cooker to the power supply. The appliance must be earthed.

Manufacturers' instructions are the best guide if good results are to be obtained. There are however general instructions for use and certain basic rules which apply to all types of Slo-Cooker.

GENERAL METHOD OF USE

1. Pre-heat the Slo-Cooker if necessary (check with your instruction book) with the lid on. Meanwhile prepare the ingredients. Preparation may include sautéeing meat and vegetables and thickening and heating liquid.

2. Place the ingredients in the Slo-Cooker. It may be filled to within $\frac{1}{2}$–1 inch (1–2$\frac{1}{2}$ cm.) of the top of the earthenware pot.

3. Replace the lid and select the heat setting recommended in the recipe. Where recipes recommend cooking on High for 20–30 minutes before turning to Low, use the Auto setting instead, if available.

4. The Slo-Cooker may now be left for the remaining cooking period.

It is important that the lid remains in position throughout cooking. If it is removed the water seal around the rim is broken and a considerable time is taken to regain the heat lost. So do resist peeping!

When cooking is completed, leftover food should always be removed from the Slo-Cooker, cooled and refrigerated or frozen. Never leave uncooked food in the Slo-Cooker to be switched on later. Ingredients prepared in advance should be stored in a separate container in the refrigerator. Cooked food, normally served hot, should not be re-heated in the Slo-Cooker.

The heat settings available on your Slo-Cooker mean that cooking times can often be adjusted to suit your lifestyle. Generally the cooking time on High is just over half that on Low. So, if a recipe in this book is meant to be cooked for 8 hours on Low and you require the finished dish earlier, cook for 5 hours on the High setting.

Cooking times can be affected by direct draughts and cold room temperatures, and these should be avoided whenever possible. In winter when the house is empty during the day, slightly longer cooking times may be necessary, especially when cooking on the Low setting. Voltage reductions in your electricity supply can also affect cooking times slightly. These uncontrollable variations usually occur during peak cooking times and during very cold weather. If a recipe is not ready at the end of the cooking period, simply replace the lid and cook for at least another hour on High.

Remember that the temperatures achieved in the Slo-Cooker are high enough to cook the food but they do not compare with even the lowest temperature of a conventional oven. Therefore, if you are adapting a recipe for the Slo-Cooker and it is normally cooked in a hot oven, this does *not* mean that it should be cooked on High in the Slo-Cooker.

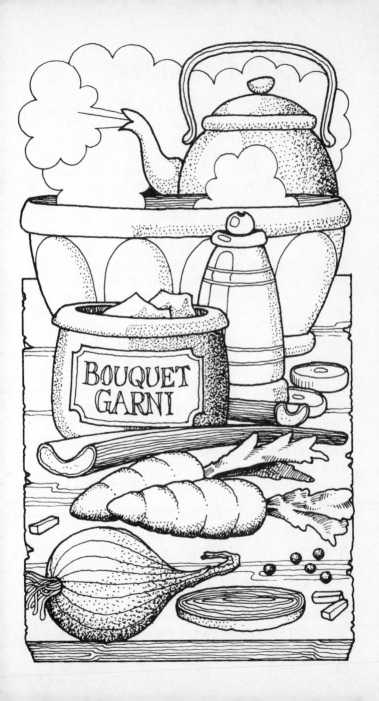

SOUPS AND STARTERS

Soups are ideal for all-day gentle simmering. There is no need to worry if they cook for a few hours longer than the recommended cooking period. The result will still be delicious—perfectly cooked and tasty, the flavours from each ingredient having developed and intermingled gently for hours.

The soups included in this section can introduce a meal delicately or they can make a meal in themselves served with crusty fresh bread and cheese.

The flavour of stock and soup prepared in a Slo-Cooker is more concentrated than that of one cooked in a saucepan in the conventional method. Remember to use leftover vegetables and bones to slow cook the basis of a good soup, casserole or stew.

Adapt any of your own favourite recipes for slow cooking and appreciate the new, richer flavour. Experiment with different herbs and spices—they cannot be spoiled.

The gentle heat of the Slo-Cooker is perfect for cooking pâtés. The slow cooked pâté is firm without being tough, with a smooth texture and a delicate blend of flavours. The Slo-Cooker can also be very versatile when an oven is not available, in a bedsitter for example. For this reason Eggs Florentine has been included in this section. All you need is a cooking plate or burner.

YOUR FREEZER AND SLOW COOKED SOUPS AND STARTERS

Soups freeze extremely well so it is a simple matter to increase quantities when cooking in your Slo-Cooker. Eat some and freeze some in suitable amounts.

Stocks can be frozen in handy blocks for adding flavour to dishes at a later date.

Pâtés are best frozen in individual serving quantities interleaved with foil or greaseproof paper and over-wrapped with foil. Then just take out as much as you need and defrost in room temperature.

CHECKPOINTS FOR SLOW COOKING SOUPS

Remember that vegetables need longer cooking than meat so they should be cut up into fairly small pieces.

Extra flavour is added to soup if meat is browned lightly in a frying pan and vegetables gently sautéed for a few minutes. The final colour of the soup will be more attractive too.

Slow cooked soups usually require less seasoning since the ingredients retain more of their own concentrated flavours.

Thickening agents: flour or cornflour may be incorporated at the start of cooking or for the final $1-1\frac{1}{2}$ hours of cooking (see the instructions on page 12). Cream, milk and egg yolks should be added during the final $\frac{1}{2}$ hour of cooking.

When adapting your own soup recipes for slow cooking, remember to use less liquid since little evaporation takes place. A good guide is to halve the quantity, then if liked, extra hot liquid can be added before serving.

Stock

INGREDIENTS	Imperial	Metric	American
Bones, raw or cooked	3–4 lb.	1.4–1.8 kg.	3–4 lb.
Onion, chopped	1	1	1
Carrot, chopped	1	1	1
Celery stick or stalk, chopped	1	1	1
Black peppercorns			
Salt			
Bouquet garni	1	1	1
Boiling water			

Pre-heat Slo-Cooker on High.
Break up the bones as small as possible to extract the most flavour. Place all ingredients in the Slo-Cooker with sufficient boiling water to cover. Cook on Low for 10–16 hours. Strain the stock. When cool skim off surface fat.

COOKING TIME
Pre-heat while preparing ingredients.
Low 10–16 hours

TO FREEZE
Pour stock into rigid polythene containers in suitable quantities for use, cover and freeze.

CHECKPOINT
The basic method for making stock is given. Most bones can of course be replaced with a poultry carcass (uncooked), skin and giblets, fish trimmings (with a little lemon peel), or washed vegetable peelings, such as carrot, mushroom, turnip, etc (but not green vegetables).

Beef Broth

 Serves 6–8

INGREDIENTS

	Imperial	Metric	American
Cooking oil	1 tbsp.	15 ml.	1 tbsp.
Stewing steak, finely chopped	8 oz.	225 g.	½ lb.
Onions, diced	8 oz.	225 g.	½ lb.
Carrots, diced	8 oz.	225 g.	½ lb.
Potatoes, diced	8 oz.	225 g.	½ lb.
Leeks, thinly sliced	1	1	1
Flour	1 tbsp. rounded	1 tbsp. rounded	1 tbsp. rounded
Beef stock	2 pt.	1.1 litre	5 cups
Pearl barley	1 oz.	25 g.	1 oz.
Salt and pepper			

Pre-heat Slo-Cooker on High.
Heat the cooking oil in a large pan and brown the
meat gently on all sides. Transfer to Slo-Cooker. In
the same oil sauté the vegetables gently for 3–4
minutes. Stir in the flour then gradually add the
stock, stirring well. Add barley and season well.
Bring to the boil then transfer to Slo-Cooker and
stir the mixture well. Cook on Low for 6–10 hours.
Stir well before serving.

COOKING TIME
Pre-heat while preparing ingredients.
Low 6–10 hours

TO FREEZE
Pack into rigid polythene container, cover and
freeze.

Pea Soup

 Serves 6–8

INGREDIENTS

	Imperial	Metric	American
Split peas	8 oz.	225 g.	½ lb.
Bicarbonate of soda	1 tsp.	1 tsp.	1 tsp.
Butter	1 oz.	25 g.	2 tbsp.
Rashers or slices of streaky bacon, chopped	4	4	4
Leek, chopped	1	1	1
Sticks or stalks of celery chopped	1 small	1 small	1 small
Chicken stock	1¾ pt.	1 litre	4½ cups
Salt and black pepper			

Soak the peas in plenty of water with the bicarbonate of soda for 5–6 hours, or overnight.

Pre-heat Slo-Cooker on High.

Heat the butter in a large pan and sauté the bacon, leek and celery gently for 3–4 minutes. Stir in the drained peas and chicken stock. Season well. Bring to the boil and transfer to Slo-Cooker. Cook on Low for 8–10 hours. Liquidise or mash the soup and reheat before serving.

COOKING TIME
Pre-heat while preparing ingredients.
Low 8–10 hours

TO FREEZE
Pack into rigid polythene container, cover and freeze.

French Onion Soup

 Serves 6

INGREDIENTS

	Imperial	Metric	American
Butter	1½ oz.	40 g.	3 tbsp.
Onions, thinly sliced	1½ lb.	700 g.	1½ lb.
Chicken stock	1½ pt.	1 litre	3¾ cups
Salt			
Black pepper			
Bay leaf			

Pre-heat Slo-Cooker on High.
Heat the butter in a large pan and sauté the onions gently till they begin to turn golden brown. Stir in the stock, season with salt and pepper and add the bay leaf. Bring to the boil then transfer to Slo-Cooker. Cook on Low for 6–8 hours. Remove bay leaf. Serve with thick slices of crusty French bread and cheese.

COOKING TIME
Pre-heat while preparing ingredients.
Low 6–8 hours

TO FREEZE
Pack into rigid polythene container, cover and freeze.
Note: If preferred, this soup may be liquidised for a smoother consistency. To make Cream of Onion Soup, stir in ¼pt/150ml/⅔ cup double (thick) cream to the liquidised mixture, re-heat but do not boil.

Lentil Soup

 Serves 6

INGREDIENTS	Imperial	Metric	American
Butter	1 oz.	25 g.	2 tbsp.
Rashers or slices of streaky bacon, chopped	4	4	4
Onions, chopped	2	2	2
Carrots, chopped	2–3	2–3	2–3
Celery sticks or stalks, chopped	2	2	2
Water	2 pt.	1.1 litre	5 cups
Tomato purée or paste	1 tbsp.	1 tbsp.	1 tbsp.
Bouquet garni			
Lentils	8 oz.	225 g.	½ lb.

Pre-heat Slo-Cooker on High.
Heat the butter in a large pan and saute the bacon, onions, carrots and celery gently for 3–4 minutes. Add remaining ingredients. Bring to the boil then transfer to Slo-Cooker. Cook on Low for 6–8 hours. Remove bouquet garni. Liquidise or sieve the soup and reheat to serve.

COOKING TIME
Pre-heat while preparing ingredients.
Low 6–8 hours

TO FREEZE
Pack into rigid polythene container, cover and freeze.

Tomato Soup

 Serves 6–8

INGREDIENTS

	Imperial	Metric	American
Butter	1 oz.	25 g.	2 tbsp.
Onion, finely chopped	1	1	1
Carrot, finely chopped	1	1	1
Sticks or stalks of celery, finely chopped	2	2	2
Rashers or slices of streaky bacon, chopped	4	4	4
Tomatoes, skinned	1½ lb.	700 g.	1½ lb.
Chicken or onion stock	1½ pt.	900 ml.	3¾ cups
Sugar	1 tsp.	1 tsp.	1 tsp.
Good pinch mixed herbs			
Salt and pepper			

Pre-heat Slo-Cooker on High.
Heat the butter in a large pan and sauté the onion, carrot, celery and bacon gently for 3–4 minutes. Stir in the remaining ingredients, bring to the boil, then transfer to Slo-Cooker. Cook on Low for 8–10 hours. Stir well before serving.

COOKING TIME
Pre-heat while preparing ingredients.
Low 8–10 hours

TO FREEZE
Pack into rigid polythene container, cover and freeze.
Note: if preferred, this soup may be liquidised for a smoother consistency. To make Cream of Tomato Soup, stir in ¼pt./150ml/⅔ cup double (thick) cream to the liquidised mixture. Reheat (without boiling).

Vichyssoise

 Serves 6

INGREDIENTS	Imperial	Metric	American
Butter	2 oz.	50 g.	$\frac{1}{4}$ cup
Onions, chopped	2	2	2
Clove garlic, crushed	1 small	1 small	1 small
Leeks, thinly sliced	1$\frac{1}{2}$ lb.	675 g.	1$\frac{1}{2}$ lb.
Potatoes, chopped	2	2	2
Salt and pepper			
Chicken stock	1$\frac{1}{2}$ pt.	900 ml.	3$\frac{3}{4}$ cups
Double cream or thick cream			
Chopped chives			

Pre-heat Slo-Cooker on High.
Heat the butter in a large pan and sauté the onions, garlic and leeks gently for 3–4 minutes. Add the potatoes, seasoning and chicken stock. Bring to the boil then transfer to Slo-Cooker. Cook on Low for 8–10 hours. Liquidise the soup. Serve chilled. To garnish stir in a little double cream and top with chopped chives.

COOKING TIME
Pre-heat while preparing ingredients.
Low 8–10 hours

TO FREEZE
Omit garlic, pack into rigid polythene containers, cover and freeze. Season with garlic or garlic salt at reheating stage.
Note: If you want a pure white soup then you should use only the white part of the leeks.

Watercress Soup

 Serves 4–6

INGREDIENTS	Imperial	Metric	American
Butter	*2 oz.*	*50 g.*	*¼ cup*
Onion, finely chopped	*1*	*1*	*1*
Bunches watercress	*2*	*2*	*2*
Chicken stock	*1 pt.*	*600 ml.*	*2½ cups*
Salt and pepper			
Milk	*½ pt*	*300 ml.*	*1¼ cups*

Pre-heat Slo-Cooker on High.
Heat the butter in a large pan and sauté the onion
gently until transparent. Stir in the washed
watercress and cook for a further 2–3 minutes,
stirring all the time. Add the stock and seasoning
and bring to the boil. Transfer to Slo-Cooker. Cook
on Low for 6–8 hours, liquidise the soup, stir in the
milk and reheat to serve. Garnish with a few
watercress leaves.

COOKING TIME
Pre-heat while preparing ingredients.
Low 6–8 hours

TO FREEZE
Omit milk. Pack liquidised soup into rigid
polythene container, cover and freeze. Stir in milk
on reheating.

Spinach and Celery Soup

 Serves 6

INGREDIENTS	Imperial	Metric	American
Butter	*1 oz.*	*25 g.*	*2 tbsp.*
Celery, chopped	*1 small head*	*1 small head*	*1 small head*
Onion, chopped	*1*	*1*	*1*
Spinach, roughly chopped	*1 lb.*	*450 g.*	*1 lb.*
Water	*1½ pt.*	*900 ml.*	*3¾ cup*
Salt			
Freshly ground black pepper			
Milk	*¼ pt.*	*150 ml.*	*⅔ cup*
Double cream or thick cream			

Pre-heat Slo-Cooker on **High**.
Heat the butter in a large pan and sauté the celery and onions, gently for a few minutes. Add the spinach, water, salt and pepper and bring to the boil. Transfer to Slo-Cooker. Cook on Low for 6–10 hours. Liquidise the soup, stir in the milk, reheat and serve with a swirl of double cream.

COOKING TIME
Pre-heat while preparing ingredients.
Low 6–10 hours

TO FREEZE
Omit milk, pack into rigid polythene container, cover and freeze. Add milk at reheating stage.

Cucumber and Mint Soup

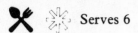 Serves 6

INGREDIENTS	Imperial	Metric	American
Butter	1 oz.	25 g.	2 tbsp.
Onion, chopped	1	1	1
Cucumber, peeled and sliced	1 large	1 large	1 large
Chicken stock	1 pt.	600 ml.	2½ cups
Mint, chopped fresh or	2 tbsp.	2 tbsp.	2 tbsp.
Dried mint	1 tbsp.	1 tbsp.	1 tbsp.
Salt and pepper			
Milk	½ pt.	300 ml.	1¼ cups
Carton natural unsweetened yoghurt	1 small	1 small	1 small

Pre-heat Slo-Cooker on High.
In a large pan heat the butter and sauté the onion until transparent. Stir in the cucumber, chicken stock, mint and seasoning and bring to the boil. Transfer to Slo-Cooker. Cook on Low for 4–8 hours. Liquidise the soup, stir in the milk and chill. Serve in chilled bowls with a little yoghurt stirred in each.

COOKING TIME
Pre-heat while preparing ingredients.
Low 4–8 hours

TO FREEZE
Omit milk, pour into rigid polythene container, cover and freeze.
Note: This soup may also be served hot with croutons.

Winter Vegetable Soup

 Serves 6

INGREDIENTS

	Imperial	Metric	American
Butter	2 oz.	50 g.	$\frac{1}{4}$ cup
Onions, chopped	8 oz.	225 g.	$\frac{1}{2}$ lb.
Carrots, diced	8 oz.	225 g.	$\frac{1}{2}$ lb.
Parsnips, diced	8 oz.	225 g.	$\frac{1}{2}$ lb.
Celery sticks or stalks, chopped	2	2	2
Tomatoes, skinned and chopped	8 oz.	225 g.	$\frac{1}{2}$ lb.
Flour	3 tbsp.	3 tbsp.	3 tbsp.
Stock	$1\frac{1}{2}$ pt.	1 litre	$3\frac{3}{4}$ cup
Bouquet garni			
Salt and pepper			

Pre-heat Slo-Cooker on High.
Heat the butter in a large pan and sauté the onions,
carrots, parsnips and celery gently for about 5
minutes. Stir in the tomatoes. Mix the flour with
a little cold stock to form a smooth paste then add
this, the remaining stock and bouquet garni to the
mixture. Season well. Bring to the boil and transfer
to Slo-Cooker. Cook on Low for 6–10 hours. Remove
bouquet garni. Serve with baked potatoes and cheese
to make a filling meal.

COOKING TIME
Pre-heat while preparing ingredients.
Low 6–10 hours

CHECKPOINT
This soup may be made using other selections
of winter vegetables. Use your favourite herbs to add
interest replacing the bouquet garni.

Eggs Florentine

 Serves 4

INGREDIENTS	Imperial	Metric	American
Butter	*1 oz.*	*25 g.*	*2 tbsp.*
Spinach, washed and roughly chopped	*1 lb.*	*450 g.*	*1 lb.*
Eggs	*4*	*4*	*4*
Sauce :			
Butter	*1 oz.*	*25 g.*	*2 tbsp.*
Flour	*1 oz.*	*25 g.*	*¼ cup*
Milk	*½ pt.*	*300 ml.*	*1¼ cup*
Salt and pepper			
Cheese, finely grated			

Butter the inside of the Slo-Cooker and pre-heat on High. Arrange the roughly chopped spinach in the Slo-Cooker and cook on High for 1 hour.

To make sauce: Heat the butter in a saucepan and stir in the flour. Cook gently for 2–3 minutes. Gradually add the milk, stirring continuously, and bring to the boil. Season well. Use the base of a cup to make four depressions in the spinach. Break one egg into each. Pour the prepared sauce over, then cook on High for a further 2 hours. Sprinkle with a little grated cheese to serve.

COOKING TIME
Pre-heat while preparing ingredients.
High 1 hour and 2 hours

Fish

Fish cooked in the Slo-Cooker retains every bit of its delicate flavour. Though it is not suitable for all-day cooking I am sure you will wish to try it. Once tasted, slow cooked fish is not forgotten.

Another advantage of preparing fish in the Slo-Cooker is that it remains beautifully whole. The moist heat is so gentle that whole fish or fish pieces do not disintegrate. Treat yourself to Lemon Plaice and appreciate what I mean.

Slow cooking also takes away the exact timing normally necessary with fish cookery, though timing is of course more crucial than, say, slow cooking soups or meat.

By using the minimum amount of liquid to cook the fish and by using the cooking liquor to form a sauce, no flavour is discarded.

I hope you enjoy the following recipes. Do remember that where a white fish is included in a recipe, for example, it will taste just as good if replaced with another (perhaps a family favourite or a less expensive variety).

YOUR FREEZER AND SLOW COOKED FISH

If fish is to be appreciated at its best, it should be eaten as soon as it is cooked. I therefore do not consider it worthwhile freezing any of the recipes in the next few pages.

Frozen fish should be thawed before slow cooking.

CHECKPOINTS FOR SLOW COOKING FISH

Prepare the fish in the usual way—clean, trim, wash and season.

Cooking time will depend on the type of fish and its preparation (whole, fillets, steaks or cubes). When in doubt consult a similar recipe in this chapter or in your manufacturer's instruction book.

Do not attempt to put too many whole fish in the Slo-Cooker or the weight of the top ones could affect the finished appearance and texture of those at the bottom. Four is an ideal quantity.

Liquids used may be stock, water, wine, cider or fruit juice. Use small quantities only to retain the most fish flavour.

Thickening agents such as flour and cornflour are best added to casserole-type dishes before slow cooking. Use the method given in the recipes that follow. Where a sauce is to accompany whole fish you may prefer to thicken after cooking. Place the cooked fish on a serving dish and keep warm, then transfer the cooking liquor to a saucepan for speedy thickening with flour, cornflour, cream etc.

Cream, milk and egg yolks should be added to the Slo-Cooker during the final $\frac{1}{2}$ hour of the cooking period.

When adapting your own recipes for slow cooking consult the recipes that follow for guidance. Remember you will probably need less liquid—you can always add a little extra just before serving.

Fish Bake

 Serves 4

INGREDIENTS	Imperial	Metric	American
Butter	1 oz.	25 g.	2 tbsp.
Onion, finely chopped	1	1	1
Mackerel fillets, skinned and cubed	1 lb.	450 g.	1 lb.
Cod fillets, skinned and cubed	1 lb.	450 g.	1 lb.
Button mushrooms, sliced	4 oz.	100 g.	$\frac{1}{4}$ lb.
Tomatoes, skinned and sliced	8 oz.	225 g.	$\frac{1}{2}$ lb.
Juice 1 lemon			
Salt			
Black pepper			
Water	2–3 tbsp.	2–3 tbsp.	2–3 tbsp.

Pre-heat Slo-Cooker on High.
Heat the butter in a large pan and sauté the onion gently until transparent. Stir in the remaining ingredients, bring to the boil and transfer to Slo-Cooker. Cook on Low for 2–4 hours. Serve with triangles of fried bread.

COOKING TIME
Pre-heat while preparing ingredients.
Low 2–4 hours

Note: If your Slo-Cooker has a removable pot a topping of creamed or sliced potatoes can be added and crisped in the oven or under a hot grill.

Fish Casserole

 Serves 4

INGREDIENTS	Imperial	Metric	American
White fish, such as cod or haddock, cut into cubes	*1¼ lb.*	*675 g.*	*1¼ lb.*
Cornflour or cornstarch	*1 tbsp.*	*1 tbsp.*	*1 tbsp.*
Cooking oil	*1 tbsp.*	*15 ml.*	*1 tbsp.*
Onion, finely chopped	*1*	*1*	*1*
Courgettes, thinly sliced	*8 oz.*	*225 g.*	*½ lb.*
Dry white wine or cider	*½ pt.*	*300 ml.*	*1¼ cups*
Bay leaf			
Bouquet garni			

Pre-heat Slo-Cooker on High.

Coat the fish with the cornflour. Heat the cooking oil in a large pan and sauté the onion and courgettes gently for 4–5 minutes. Add the wine/cider, bay leaf and bouquet garni and stir in the fish. Bring to the boil and transfer to Slo-Cooker. Cook on Low for 3–6 hours.

Remove bay leaf and bouquet garni before serving.

COOKING TIME
Pre-heat while preparing ingredients.
Low 3–6 hours

Haddock and Eggs

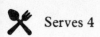 Serves 4

INGREDIENTS

	Imperial	Metric	American
Butter	1 oz.	25 g.	2 tbsp.
Smoked haddock	1½ lb.	700 g.	1½ lb.
cut into 4 pieces			
Pepper			
Milk and water			
Eggs	4	4	4

Butter the inside of the Slo-Cooker and pre-heat on High.

Arrange the haddock pieces in the Slo-Cooker and pour over sufficient milk and water (equal quantities) to just cover. Season with pepper. Cook on Low for 2 hours. Crack the eggs over the fish and continue to cook on Low for 1 further hour. Serve immediately.

COOKING TIME
Pre-heat while preparing ingredients.
Low 2 hours + 1 hour

Prawn Rissotto

 Serves 4

INGREDIENTS	Imperial	Metric	American
Cooking oil	1 tbsp.	15 ml.	1 tbsp.
Onions, finely chopped	2	2	2
Chicken stock	1½ pt.	900 ml.	3¾ cups
Button mushrooms, sliced	8 oz.	225 g.	½ lb.
Green pepper, de-seeded and chopped	1	1	1
Tomatoes, skinned and sliced	2	2	2
Easy-cook long grain rice	6 oz.	175 g.	1 cup, generous
Prawns	8 oz.	225 g.	½ lb.

Pre-heat Slo-Cooker on High.
Heat the cooking oil in a large pan and sauté the onions gently until transparent. Add the chicken stock, mushrooms and green pepper. Bring to the boil then transfer to Slo-Cooker. Stir in the tomatoes, rice and prawns. Cook on Low for 3–4 hours. Stir and serve immediately, adjusting seasoning if necessary.

COOKING TIME
Pre-heat while preparing ingredients.
Low 3–4 hours

MEAT

Your Slo-Cooker could almost have been designed specifically for cooking meat; both joints and casseroles. The recipe can be left to cook all day (and part of the evening too, if necessary) without the risk of burning or overcooking, and without the worry of checking, basting, turning or stirring. And the slow, gentle heat action tenderizes even the toughest cuts of meat.

Use the Slo-Cooker to prepare exotic, delicate recipes suitable for entertaining, as well as for tasty casseroles, stews and roasts.

Whenever possible use the juices that surround the meat as part of the meal — in the form of a rich sauce for example.

You will find that slow cooked joints of meat shrink much less than those roasted conventionally — a considerable bonus when budgeting for family meals.

YOUR FREEZER AND SLOW COOKED MEATS

The majority of slow cooked meat recipes may be frozen successfully. Specific instructions are provided in the following recipes where freezing is recommended.

Frozen meat should always be thawed completely before slow cooking. Remember though that partially frozen meat is easy to handle when chopping and slicing.

CHECKPOINTS FOR SLOW COOKING MEATS

Trim excess fat from meat.
To improve the flavour, and appearance of joints

and casserole-type dishes, lightly brown the meat in a separate pan before slow cooking.

Vegetables tend to need longer cooking than meat so cut them into small pieces (see page 14) and ensure they are immersed in the cooking liquid.

When adapting your own recipes for slow cooking reduce the quantity of liquid by approximately half. The consistency can be adjusted if necessary before serving.

Liquids may be stock, water, wine, cider, beer or fruit juice.

Be sparing with seasoning, adjust before serving.

Casseroles and stews may be thickened before slow cooking. Some gravies are thickened after cooking. Flour or cornflour is mixed with a little cold water or stock then added to the Slo-Cooker during the final 30 minutes of cooking. Alternatively, gravy or sauce may be thickened in a separate pan just before serving.

Add cream, milk, and egg yolks during the final 30 minutes of cooking.

If you have a Slo-Cooker with a removable pot, pastry and scone toppings can be added and finished off in the oven for final cooking.

When adapting recipes for slow cooking consult similar ones within this section for guidance on cooking times.

Cooking times for joints vary according to size, shape, quality, the proportions of meat, fat and bone and personal tastes Use the following times for guidance. . . .

Roast joints on High setting for: 3–6 hours (3–5 hours High for pork) if 2–3½ lb. (1–1.6 kg.); 5–8 hours (4–6 hours High for pork) if 3½–5 lb. (1.6–2.3 kg.).

If a crisp skin is required when cooking a pork joint, do not fry the joint before slow cooking. When the joint is cooked grill the skin side for about 10 minutes to crisp.

Beef Goulash

 Serves 6

INGREDIENTS

	Imperial	Metric	American
Stewing steak, cut into cubes	2½ lb.	1 kg.	2½ lb.
Seasoned flour	3–4 tbsp.	3–4 tbsp.	3–4 tbsp.
Cooking oil	3 tbsp.	3 tbsp.	3 tbsp.
Onions, chopped	3	3	3
Green peppers, de-seeded and sliced	2	2	2
Beef stock	½ pt.	300 ml.	1¼ cups
Canned tomatoes	14 oz.	397 g.	1 lb.
Tomato purée or paste	3 tbsp.	3 tbsp.	3 tbsp.
Paprika pepper	3 tsp.	3 tsp.	3 tsp.
Bouquet garni	1	1	1
For garnish:			
Sour cream or natural, unsweetened yoghurt			

Pre-heat Slo-Cooker on High.

Coat the meat with seasoned flour. Heat the cooking oil in a large pan and brown the meat lightly. Stir in the onions and peppers and cook for a further 2–3 minutes. Add the remaining ingredients, except cream, bring to the boil and transfer to Slo-Cooker. Cook on Low for 7–10 hours. Before serving, remove bouquet garni, adjust seasoning if necessary and stir the Goulash well.

Add a swirl of soured cream or yoghurt. This dish is superb served simply with dressed salad.

COOKING TIME
Pre-heat while preparing ingredients.
Low 7–10 hours

Pork in Cider

 Serves 4

INGREDIENTS

	Imperial	Metric	American
Cooking oil	1 tbsp.	15 ml.	1 tbsp.
Butter	1 oz.	25 g.	2 tbsp.
Onion, sliced	1	1	1
Sticks or stalks celery, sliced	2	2	2
Cooking apple, peeled, cored and chopped	1 large	1 large	1 large
Lean pork such as shoulder, cut in cubes	1¾ lb.	800 g.	1¾ lb.
Flour	2 tbsp.	2 tbsp.	2 tbsp.
Dry cider	½ pt.	300 ml.	1¼ cups
Salt and pepper			
Bouquet garni			

Pre-heat Slo-Cooker on High.
Heat the cooking oil and butter in a large pan and sauté the onion, celery and apple gently for 2–3 minutes. Transfer to Slo-Cooker. In the same pan brown the pork lightly. Mix the flour with a little dry cider then stir in the rest. Add this to the pork along with salt and black pepper and bouquet garni. Bring to the boil, stirring well. Transfer to Slo-Cooker and stir the mixture. Cook on Low for 6–10 hours. Remove bouquet garni before serving.

COOKING TIME
Pre-heat while preparing ingredients.
Low 6–10 hours

TO FREEZE
Pack into rigid polythene or foil container, cover and freeze.

Lamb Cutlets in Red Wine Sauce

 Serves 4

INGREDIENTS	Imperial	Metric	American
Cooking oil	2 tbsp.	30 ml.	2 tbsp.
Onions, cut into fine rings	2	2	2
Salt and pepper			
Lamb cutlets	8	8	8
Cornflour or cornstarch	1 tbsp.	1 tbsp.	1 tbsp.
Red wine	½ pt.	300 ml.	1¼ cups
Dried rosemary	2 tsp.	2 tsp.	2 tsp.

Pre-heat Slo-Cooker on High.

Heat the cooking oil in a large pan and sauté the onions gently till beginning to turn transparent. Transfer to Slo-Cooker. Season the lamb cutlets with salt and pepper and brown all sides quickly in the same pan. Arrange on top of the onions in the Slo-Cooker. Mix the cornflour into the remaining fat in the pan, then slowly add the red wine, stirring well. Add the rosemary. Bring to the boil, pour the sauce over the cutlets in the Slo-Cooker. Cook on Low for 4–6 hours.

COOKING TIME
Pre-heat while preparing ingredients.
Low 4–6 hours

Navarin of Lamb

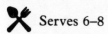 Serves 6–8

INGREDIENTS

	Imperial	Metric	American
Best end neck lamb chops	2½ lb.	1 kg.	2½ lb.
Salt and pepper			
Butter	½ oz.	15 g.	1 tbsp.
Carrots, sliced	3 large	3 large	3 large
Onions, chopped	2	2	2
Potatoes, cut in ½ in. (1 cm.) cubes	1 lb.	450 g.	1 lb.
Flour	2–3 tbsp.	2–3 tbsp.	2–3 tbsp.
Beef stock	1 pt.	500 ml.	2½ cups
Sugar	2 tsp.	2 tsp.	2 tsp.
Tomato purée or paste	3 tbsp.	3 tbsp.	3 tbsp.
Bouquet garni			

Pre-heat Slo-Cooker on High.
Season the lamb chops with salt and pepper. Heat the butter in a large pan and brown the chops quickly on all sides. Transfer to Slo-Cooker. In the same pan, sauté the vegetables gently for 3–4 minutes. Mix the flour first with a little beef stock, then the remainder. Add this and the remaining ingredients to the vegetables. Bring to the boil, stirring continuously. Transfer to Slo-Cooker and stir well. Cook on Low for 7–10 hours.

Remove bouquet garni before serving and adjust seasoning if necessary.

COOKING TIME
Pre-heat while preparing ingredients.
Low 7–10 hours

Piquant Bacon

 Serves 6

INGREDIENTS	Imperial	Metric	American
Unsmoked bacon, cut into cubes	2½ lb.	1 kg.	2½ lb.
Butter	2 oz.	50 g.	¼ cup
Onion, chopped	1 large	1 large	1 large
Carrots, sliced	2	2	2
Flour	2 tbsp.	2 tbsp.	2 tbsp.
Chicken stock or white wine	½ pt.	300 ml.	1¼ cups
Vinegar	3 tbsp.	3 tbsp.	3 tbsp.
Black pepper	½ tsp.	½ tsp.	½ tsp.
Ground cloves	pinch	pinch	pinch

Pre-heat Slo-Cooker on High.
Place the bacon cubes in a large pan and cover with cold water. Bring slowly to the boil. Discard the water and dry the bacon on kitchen paper. Heat the butter in a large pan and brown the bacon lightly. Transfer to Slo-Cooker. In the same butter sauté the onion and carrots for 2–3 minutes. Stir in the flour then gradually add the chicken stock/wine and vinegar. Bring to the boil and add the pepper and cloves. Transfer to Slo-Cooker and stir the mixture well. Cook on Low for 7–10 hours.

COOKING TIME
Pre-heat while preparing ingredients.
Low 7–10 hours

TO FREEZE
Pack into rigid polythene or foil container, cover and freeze.

Pork and Pineapple Curry

 Serves 6

INGREDIENTS	Imperial	Metric	American
Flour	1½ oz.	40 g.	⅓ cup
Salt	1 tsp.	1 tsp.	1 tsp.
Lean pork, cut into cubes	2 lb.	1 kg.	2 lb.
Cooking oil	2 tbsp.	2 tbsp.	2 tbsp
Onion, finely chopped	1 large	1 large	1 large
Curry powder	1 tbsp.	1 tbsp.	1 tbsp.
Paprika pepper	1 tbsp.	1 tbsp.	1 tbsp.
Chicken stock	½ pt.	300 ml.	1¼ cups
Dried red chillies	2	2	2
Mango chutney	1 tbsp.	1 tbsp.	1 tbsp.
Worcestershire sauce	1 tsp.	1 tsp.	1 tsp.
Canned pineapple cubes, including syrup	1 lb.	450 g.	1 lb.
Bay leaves	2	2	2

Pre-heat Slo-Cooker on High.

Mix together the flour and salt then toss the pork pieces till coated. Heat the cooking oil in a large pan and brown the meat gently on all sides. Transfer to Slo-Cooker. In the same oil sauté the onion until soft. Add the remaining ingredients, bring to the boil and transfer to Slo-Cooker. Stir the curry well. Cook on Low for 5–8 hours. Remove bay leaves and stir well before serving with boiled rice.

COOKING TIME
Pre-heat while preparing ingredients.
Low 5–8 hours

Veal and Tomato Casserole

 Serves 4

INGREDIENTS

	Imperial	Metric	American
Cooking oil	2 tbsp.	30 ml.	2 tbsp.
Clove garlic, crushed	1	1	1
Lemon juice	2 tbsp.	30 ml.	2 tbsp.
Salt			
Freshly ground black pepper			
Thyme, dried	¼ tsp.	¼ tsp.	¼ tsp.
Stewing veal, cut into cubes	1½ lb.	700 g.	1½ lb.
Flour	2 tbsp.	2 tbsp.	2 tbsp.
Dry white wine	¼ pt.	150 ml.	⅔ cup
Canned tomatoes	14 oz.	397 g.	medium can

Mix together the cooking oil, garlic, lemon juice, salt, pepper and thyme, and use to coat the veal cubes. Leave the mixture to marinate for ½–1 hour, turning occasionally. **Pre-heat Slo-Cooker on High.**

In a saucepan, mix the flour with the white wine to form a smooth paste. Stir in the tomatoes (including juice) and the veal mixture. Bring to the boil, stirring continuously. Transfer to Slo-Cooker. Cook on Low for 7–10 hours. Stir before serving and adjust seasoning if necessary.

COOKING TIME
Pre-heat while preparing ingredients.
Low 7–10 hours

TO FREEZE
Pack into rigid polythene or foil container, cover and freeze.

Braised Oxtail

 Serves 4

INGREDIENTS

	Imperial	Metric	American
Cooking oil	2 tbsp.	30 ml.	2 tbsp.
Streaky bacon	4 oz.	100 g.	¼ lb.
Onion, finely sliced	1 large	1 large	1 large
Carrots, thinly sliced	8 oz.	225 g.	½ lb.
Oxtail joints	2 lb.	900 g.	2 lb.
Seasoned flour			
Beef stock	1 pt.	600 ml.	2½ cups
Bouquet garni			
Redcurrant jelly (optional)	1 tbsp.	1 tbsp.	1 tbsp.

Pre-heat Slo-Cooker on High.
Heat the cooking oil in a large pan and sauté the bacon, onion and carrots gently for 3–4 minutes. Transfer to Slo-Cooker. Coat the oxtail joints with seasoned flour and, using the same pan, brown them on all sides. Stir in the beef stock and add the bouquet garni. Bring to the boil then transfer to Slo-Cooker. Stir well. Cook on Low for 8–10 hours. Just before serving, stir well, remove bouquet garni and add the redcurrant jelly (optional).

COOKING TIME
Pre-heat while preparing ingredients.
Low 8–10 hours

TO FREEZE
Pack into rigid polythene or foil container, cover and freeze.

Sausage Supper

 Serves 6

INGREDIENTS	Imperial	Metric	American
Cooking oil	2 tbsp.	30 ml.	2 tbsp.
Onion, chopped	1	1	1
Potatoes, thinly sliced	1 lb.	450 g.	1 lb.
Salt and black pepper			
Skinless beef sausages, cut in half	1 lb.	450 g.	1 lb.
Canned baked beans	15¾ oz.	447 g.	medium can
Mushrooms, halved	4 oz.	100 g.	¼ lb.
Chilli powder	2 tsp.	2 tsp.	2 tsp.
Tomato purée or paste	1 tbsp.	1 tbsp.	1 tbsp.
Water	¼ pt.	150 ml.	⅔ cup

Pre-heat Slo-Cooker on High.

Heat the cooking oil in a large pan and sauté the onion and potatoes gently for 4–5 minutes. Season with salt and black pepper. Add the remaining ingredients and bring to the boil. Transfer to Slo-Cooker. Cook on Low for 6–10 hours. Serve with warm crusty bread to make a filling meal.

COOKING TIME
Pre-heat while preparing ingredients.
Low 6–10 hours

Braised Danish Bacon

Serves 6

INGREDIENTS	Imperial	Metric	American
Danish bacon joint, such as prime collar or gammon	2 lb.	1 kg.	2 lb.
Brown sugar	1 tbsp.	1 tbsp.	1 tbsp.
Tomatoes, skinned and coarsely chopped	8 oz.	225 g.	½ lb.
Onions, finely sliced	8 oz.	225 g.	½ lb.
Black pepper			
Water	2 tbsp.	2 tbsp.	2 tbsp.
Mushrooms, sliced	4 oz.	100 g.	¼ lb.
Lemon juice	2 tbsp.	30 ml.	2 tbsp.
Chopped parsley			

Pre-heat Slo-Cooker on High.
Place the bacon joint in a large pan and cover with cold water. Bring slowly to the boil and pour the water away. Cut off the rind and snip into the fat at intervals. Sprinkle the joint with the brown sugar and place under a pre-heated grill to melt and brown. (If your Slo-Cooker has a removable pot this can be done in the earthenware pot.) Arrange the tomatoes and onions in layers in the Slo-Cooker. Season with black pepper and add the water. Place the browned bacon joint on top. **Cook on High for 3-5 hours.**

In a separate pan cook the mushrooms in a little water with the lemon juice for about 3 minutes. Drain and use to garnish the dish. Sprinkle chopped parsley over.

COOKING TIME
Pre-heat while preparing ingredients.
High 3-5 hours

POULTRY AND GAME

Slow cooked poultry and game is deliciously moist and tender, with none of the drying out that normally takes place during conventional cooking. Roasting birds or boiling fowl are cooked perfectly in the Slo-Cooker. The flesh of game and boiling fowl is often tough enough to require long cooking anyway, and the Slo-Cooker will tenderise gently and slowly, and all the flavour is sealed in the pot.

Whole birds and joints may be prepared in your Slo Cooker and many different recipes are given here. The size of your Slow Cooker will of course dictate the size of the bird you cook. A 4 lb. (1.8 kg) chicken fits snugly into a 4 pint (2.5 litre) pot.

Try Parsley Roast Chicken as an introduction to slow cooking poultry and taste the difference.

YOUR FREEZER AND SLOW COOKED POULTRY AND GAME

Frozen poultry and game must be completely thawed before cooking.

Poultry and game dishes are most successful freezing candidates. Special instructions are given where necessary in the following recipes.

Frozen poultry dishes are best thawed at room temperature and reheated gently in the oven just before serving.

CHECKPOINTS FOR SLOW COOKING POULTRY AND GAME

To improve the flavour and appearance of the finished dish, poultry and game require light browning in a separate pan before slow cooking.

Cut vegetables into small pieces to ensure even cooking (see page 14).

Whole poultry is best trussed for slow cooking to enable easy removal from the pot, particularly if a recipe is left to cook for longer than intended.

Always cook whole poultry on the High setting.

Avoid considerable overcooking of poultry. The flesh remains beautifully succulent and tasty of course but when the bones begin to fall apart after long cooking they can prove annoying.

When adapting your own recipes for slow cooking do not be heavy-handed with the seasoning. It is better to adjust seasoning to taste before serving.

Remember to use less liquid (about half normally) since little is lost through evaporation.

Liquids used may be stock, water, wine, cider or fruit juice.

Thickening agents such as flour or cornflour may be added to the dish at the start of cooking (as in most of the recipes to follow) or at the end (follow the instructions on page 12). Egg yolks, cream and milk should not be added till about 30 minutes before serving.

For guidance on cooking times when adapting your own recipes consult a similar recipe in this section.

The Slo-Cooker may be filled to within $\frac{1}{2}$–1 inch (1–2$\frac{1}{2}$ cm.) of the brim.

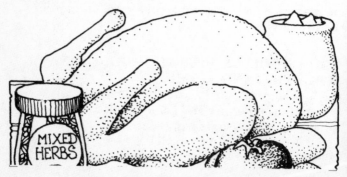

Spicy Chicken

 Serves 4

INGREDIENTS	Imperial	Metric	American
Butter	2 oz.	50 g.	¼ cup
Chicken joints	4	4	4
Onion, chopped	1	1	1
Sticks or stalks celery, chopped	2	2	2
Flour	2 tbsp.	2 tbsp.	2 tbsp.
Chicken stock	¼ pt.	150 ml.	⅔ cup
Canned pineapple pieces	15½ oz.	439 g.	medium can
Chilli powder	1½ tsp.	1½ tsp.	1½ tsp.
Ground ginger	½ tsp.	½ tsp.	½ tsp.
Salt	1 tsp.	1 tsp.	1 tsp.
Black pepper	½ tsp.	½ tsp.	½ tsp.
Tabasco sauce	few drops	few drops	few drops

Pre-heat Slo-Cooker on High.
Heat the butter in a large pan and brown the chicken joints on all sides. Transfer to Slo-Cooker. In the same butter sauté the onion and celery until beginning to turn transparent. Stir in the flour then the chicken stock slowly. Add the pineapple (including juice) and remaining ingredients. Bring to the boil, stirring continuously.

Pour this sauce over the chicken in the Slo-Cooker. Cook on Low for 5–8 hours. Serve with plenty of green salad.

COOKING TIME
Pre-heat while preparing ingredients.
Low 5–8 hours

Chicken Casserole

 Serves 4

INGREDIENTS

	Imperial	Metric	American
Butter	2 oz.	50 g.	$\frac{1}{4}$ cup
Chicken joints	4	4	4
Onions, chopped	2	2	2
Clove garlic, crushed	1	1	1
Rashers or slices streaky bacon, chopped	2	2	2
Carrots, chopped	2 large	2 large	2 large
Sticks or stalks celery, chopped	2	2	2
Flour	2 tbsp.	2 tbsp.	2 tbsp.
Chicken stock	$\frac{3}{4}$ pt.	400 ml.	2 cups
Tomato purée or paste	2 tbsp.	2 tbsp.	2 tbsp.
Salt and pepper			
Bouquet garni			
Frozen sweetcorn and peppers	8 oz.	226 g.	$\frac{1}{2}$ lb.

Pre-heat Slo-Cooker on High.
Heat the butter in a large pan and brown the chicken joints well on all sides. Transfer to Slo-Cooker. In the same butter sauté the onions, garlic, bacon, carrots and celery gently for 3–4 minutes. Stir in the flour then slowly add the chicken stock, stirring well. Add the tomato purée seasoning and bouquet garni and bring to boil, stirring continuously.

Pour the sauce over the chicken in the Slo-Cooker. Cook on Low for 6–8 hours. Remove bouquet garni and adjust seasoning if necessary. ½–1 hour before serving stir in the defrosted sweetcorn and peppers.

COOKING TIME
Pre-heat while preparing ingredients.
Low 6–8 hours

TO FREEZE
Omit garlic. Pack into rigid polythene or foil container cover and freeze. Add garlic at reheating stage, or season with garlic salt.

Coq-au-Vin

  Serves 4

INGREDIENTS	Imperial	Metric	American
Butter	*2 oz.*	*50 g.*	*¼ cup*
Chicken joints	*4*	*4*	*4*
Onion, chopped	*2*	*2*	*2*
Clove garlic, crushed	*1*	*1*	*1*
Rashers or slices streaky bacon, chopped	*6*	*6*	*6*
Flour	*2 oz.*	*50 g.*	*½ cup*
Chicken stock	*¼ pt.*	*150 ml.*	*⅔ cup*
Red wine	*½ pt.*	*300 ml.*	*1¼ cups*
Button mushrooms, halved	*4 oz.*	*100 g.*	*¼ lb.*

Salt and black pepper			
Bay leaves	2	2	2
Bouquet garni	1	1	1

Pre-heat Slo-Cooker on High.

Heat the butter in a large pan and brown the chicken joints on all sides. Transfer to Slo-Cooker. In the same butter sauté the onion, garlic and bacon gently until beginning to turn transparent. Stir in the flour then gradually add the chicken stock and red wine.

Bring to the boil, stir in the remaining ingredients then transfer to Slo-Cooker. Cook on Low for 6–8 hours. Before serving remove the bay leaves and bouquet garni.

COOKING TIME
Pre-heat while preparing ingredients.
Low 6–8 hours

TO FREEZE
Omit garlic. Pack into rigid polythene or foil container, cover and freeze. Add garlic or garlic salt at reheating stage.

Parsley Roast Chicken

 Serves 6

INGREDIENTS	Imperial	Metric	American
Roasting chicken	4 lb.	1.8 kg.	4 lb.
Clove garlic, cut into slivers	1 large	1 large	1 large
Salt			
Black pepper, freshly ground			
Cooking oil	4 tbsp.	60 ml.	4 tbsp.
Butter	4 oz.	100 g.	$\frac{1}{4}$ lb.
Chopped parsley	3 tbsp.	3 tbsp.	3 tbsp.

Pre-heat Slo-Cooker on High.
Using a sharp knife cut small slits in the breasts and thighs of the chicken and insert the slithers of garlic. Season the bird with salt and freshly ground black pepper. Heat the cooking oil and butter in a large pan and brown the chicken well on all sides. Lift into Slo-Cooker. Stir the parsley into the remaining oil and butter and use it to coat the chicken. Cook on High for 4–5 hours.

COOKING TIME
Pre-heat while preparing ingredients.
High 4–5 hours

TO FREEZE
Leftover slices or portions may be frozen in foil trays.

Turkey Supreme

 Serves 6

INGREDIENTS

	Imperial	Metric	American
Butter	1 oz.	25 g.	2 tbsp.
Turkey breasts, cut into pieces or turkey drumsticks	4 6	4 6	4 6
Onion, thinly sliced	1	1	1
Sticks or stalks celery, chopped	4	4	4
Carrots, diced	2	2	2
Flour	2 tbsp.	2 tbsp.	2 tbsp.
Chicken stock	½ pt.	300 ml.	1¼ cups
Bouquet garni			
Salt and pepper			
Single or thin cream	¼ pt.	150 ml.	⅔ cup

Pre-heat Slo-Cooker on High.

Heat the butter in a large pan and sauté the turkey gently for 2–3 minutes. Transfer to Slo-Cooker. In the same butter sauté the onion, celery and carrots for a further 2–3 minutes. Stir in the flour then gradually add the chicken stock, bouquet garni and seasoning. Bring to the boil stirring continuously and pour over the turkey. Cook on Low for 6–8 hours. 30 minutes before serving stir in the cream.

Garnish with grilled bacon rolls.

COOKING TIME
Pre-heat while preparing ingredients.
Low 6–8 hours

TO FREEZE
Omit cream, pack in rigid polythene or foil containers, cover and freeze. Add cream on reheating.

VEGETABLES

Vegetable flavours are delicate, so it is good to know that they are sealed in during slow cooking and gently but surely developed within the pot. You will probably find the texture differs slightly to vegetables cooked conventionally but you will most certainly note and appreciate the improved flavours.

Fresh, frozen, and dried vegetables are suitable for slow cooking. Refer to the following list of checkpoints for guidance.

Of the recipes in this section, some can be eaten as an appetiser, some as a main course, and others as an accompaniment to a main course. I hope you will enjoy menu-mixing and trying your own vegetable recipes in the Slo-Cooker.

YOUR FREEZER AND SLOW COOKED VEGETABLES

Frozen vegetables should be thawed before adding to the Slo-Cooker. In order to retain their full colour and texture, stir them into a recipe during the final $\frac{1}{2}$–1 hour of cooking. This will also avoid suddenly and drastically lowering the temperature within the Slo-Cooker.

Slow cooked vegetables can be frozen, particularly if cooked in a sauce, though you may not feel it is worth it for some recipes. Remember that vegetables tend to lose some of their flavour and texture on freezing and reheating. Suitable recipes for freezing have been marked in this section.

CHECKPOINTS FOR SLOW COOKING VEGETABLES

Generally speaking vegetables require long cooking times in the Slo-Cooker. It is important therefore to cut them into fairly small pieces. A thickness of ¼ inch (½ cm) is a good standard. This applies particularly when the recipe combines root vegetables and meat.

Root vegetables such as potatoes, carrots, turnips, swede, onion, etc. usually require a cooking period of at least 6 hours on Low setting.

Ensure even cooking by cutting the vegetables evenly.

Quickly-cooked vegetables can be added to a recipe ½-1 hour before serving.

Remember to include less seasoning — the vegetables will retain all their own concentrated flavour. Adjustments can always be made at the end of the cooking period.

Remember also, when adapting your own recipes for slow cooking, to reduce the amount of liquid used. It is worth noting however that some vegetables are liable to dry up on the outside and discolour if not covered with liquid. Additionally they will not cook in the recommended time. These include potatoes and other root vegetables. You will probably find you need fewer vegetables to flavour a recipe, particularly the stronger types, such as onions and leeks.

Thickening agents (flour and cornflour) can be added at the start of cooking. Add cream, milk and egg yolks during the final 30 minutes.

PULSES

If a recipe includes dried peas or beans, it is important to soak them overnight in water to help the softening process. Soaking isn't necessary for lentils. Drain and rinse the beans or peas (and especially dried red kidney beans) and BOIL them in the cooking liquid for 10 minutes before adding to the Slo-Cooker. *On no account should they be added without boiling first, nor eaten raw or undercooked.* Seasoning should be added at the end of cooking. If dried pulses are stale they will not cook successfully.

NOTE: If using canned beans or peas, drain and add 30 minutes before end of cooking time.

Pease in the Pot

 Serves 4–6

INGREDIENTS	Imperial	Metric	American
Dried peas	8 oz.	225 g.	½ lb.
Bicarbonate of soda	1 tsp.	1 tsp.	1 tsp.
Butter	1 oz.	25 g.	2 tbsp.
Streaky bacon rashers or slices chopped	4	4	4
Water	¾ pt.	400 ml.	2 cups
Salt			
Black pepper			

Soak peas overnight with the bicarbonate of soda in 1 pt./500 ml./2½ cups water.

Pre-heat Slo-Cooker on High.

Drain the peas then boil in plenty of water for 10 minutes.

Heat the butter in a pan and sauté the chopped bacon gently for 2–3 minutes. Add the drained peas, water and seasoning. Bring to the boil then transfer to Slo-Cooker. Cook on Low for 8–12 hours.

COOKING TIME
Pre-heat while preparing ingredients.
Low 8–12 hours

TO FREEZE
Pack into rigid polythene or foil container, cover and freeze.

Courgettes Hereford

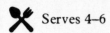 Serves 4–6

INGREDIENTS	Imperial	Metric	American
Butter	1½ oz.	40 g.	3 tbsp.
Courgettes, cut into 1 in./2½ cm lengths	1 lb.	450 g.	1 lb.
Garlic clove, crushed	1	1	1
Small onion, chopped finely	1	1	1
Cornflour or cornstarch	1 tbsp.	1 tbsp.	1 tbsp.
Apple juice	½ pt.	300 ml.	1¼ cups
Salt			
Black pepper			
Tomatoes, skinned and sliced	2–3	2–3	2–3

Pre-heat Slo-Cooker on High.

Heat the butter in a large pan and sauté the courgettes quickly till lightly browned. Transfer to Slo-Cooker. In the same fat sauté the garlic and onion gently until they begin to turn transparent. Add the cornflour then carefully stir in the apple juice. Season with salt and pepper, stir in the tomatoes, and bring to the boil (stirring continuously). Pour the sauce over the courgettes and cook on Low for 4–6 hours. The courgettes should have a slight bite.

COOKING TIME
Pre-heat while preparing ingredients.
Low 4–6 hours

Italian Stuffed Peppers

 Serves 4

INGREDIENTS	Imperial	Metric	American
Macaroni, thin-cut, quick-cook	*2 oz.*	*50 g.*	*2 oz.*
Cooking oil	*2 tbsp.*	*2 tbsp.*	*2 tbsp.*
Onion, medium diced	*1*	*1*	*1*
Clove garlic, crushed	*1*	*1*	*1*
Minced beef	*1 lb.*	*450 g.*	*1 lb.*
Flour	*2 tbsp.*	*2 tbsp.*	*2 tbsp.*
Tomato purée or paste	*2 tsp.*	*2 tsp.*	*2 tsp.*
Tomato ketchup	*2 tbsp.*	*2 tbsp.*	*2 tbsp.*
Beef stock	*¼ pt.*	*150 ml.*	*⅔ cup*
Button mushrooms, diced	*4 oz.*	*100 g.*	*~¼ lb.*
Mixed herbs	*½ tsp.*	*½ tsp.*	*½ tsp.*
Large green peppers	*4*	*4*	*4*

Pre-heat Slo-Cooker on High.
Boil the macaroni in slightly salted water until
just tender. Drain. Heat the cooking oil in a large
pan and sauté the onion and garlic until transparent.
Add the beef and continue cooking for 2–3 minutes.
Stir in the flour, tomato purée, tomato ketchup and
beef stock. Boil until thickened then add the
mushrooms, herbs and drained macaroni. Remove
the stalk and cut the cap from the top of each pepper;
remove the seeds. Fill the peppers with the beef
mixture and stand them in the Slo-Cooker. Pour
round ¼ pt./150 ml./⅔ cup slightly salted water. Cook o
Low for 5–8 hours.

COOKING TIME
Pre-heat while preparing ingredients.
Low 5–8 hours

CHECKPOINT
Do not allow the peppers to touch the walls of the Slo-Cooker as they will burn.

Tuna-stuffed Marrow

 Serves 6

INGREDIENTS	Imperial	Metric	American
Can tuna fish	*7 oz.*	*198 g.*	*medium*
Onion, finely chopped	*1*	*1*	*1*
Long-grain rice, cooked	*4 tbsp.*	*4 tbsp.*	*4 tbsp.*
Salt and pepper			
Chopped parsley	*1 tbsp.*	*1 tbsp.*	*1 tbsp.*
Juice of lemon	*½*	*½*	*½*
Marrow, medium-large	*1*	*1*	*1*

Pre-heat Slo-Cooker on High.

Drain and flake the tuna fish and mix with the onion, rice, seasoning, parsley and lemon juice. Cut off the ends of the marrow and trim the length so that it will stand upright in the Slo-Cooker. Scoop out the seeds using a spoon. Fill the marrow with the fish mixture and wrap it in buttered foil. Stand the marrow in the Slo-Cooker and pour round ½ pt./300 ml./1¼ cups boiling water. Cook on Low for 8–10 hours. Serve with tomato sauce if liked.

COOKING TIME
Pre-heat while preparing ingredients.
Low 8–10 hours

Greek Mushrooms

 Serves 8

INGREDIENTS	Imperial	Metric	American
Cooking oil	2 tbsp.	2 tbsp.	2 tbsp.
Onion, finely chopped	1	1	1
Clove garlic, crushed	1	1	1
Button mushrooms	1½ lb.	700 g.	1½ lb.
Canned tomatoes	10 oz.	397 g.	medium can
Salt	2 tsp.	2 tsp.	2 tsp.
Black pepper, freshly ground			
Chopped parsley			

Pre-heat Slo-Cooker on High.

Heat the cooking oil in a large pan and sauté the onion and garlic gently until beginning to turn transparent. Add the mushrooms, tomatoes and salt, and season to taste with black pepper. Bring to the boil and transfer to Slo-Cooker. Cook on Low for 2–3 hours. Stir in the parsley before serving.

Superb as a vegetable accompaniment or as an appetiser with hot toast or crusty bread. Can be served hot or cold.

COOKING TIME
Pre-heat while preparing ingredients.
Low 2–3 hours

TO FREEZE
Pack into rigid polythene container, cover and freeze. Thaw in room temperature.

DESSERTS

Traditional puddings and desserts are no longer just memories of childhood when you have a Slo-Cooker. Your own pudding recipes, for example, can easily be adapted for slow cooking. Just follow the recipes in this section for guidance. Timing is not nearly so crucial as with conventional cooking.

Slo-Cooked fruit is 'something special'. Its flavour is gently developed within the pot while the fruit remains beautifully whole for serving. Fruit flavours, spices etc. complement each other to produce a subtle end to a meal.

The Slo-Cooker is ideal for preparing pie, pudding and crumble fillings. Just place the fruit, water and spices in the Slo-Cooker and leave to cook while you are otherwise occupied.

Fruit and delicate desserts such as egg custard, ideally require careful, long cooking without the risk of overcooking. They are therefore perfectly suited to slow cooking since the timing is more flexible than during conventional cooking.

Cookers with removable pots facilitate the addition of a topping to be crisped up in a hot oven or under a hot grill. In Slo-Cookers with permanently fixed pots, a base (such as fruit) could be prepared in the Slo-Cooker while the cook is away from home, then finished off later in a separate dish with a meringue or crumble topping.

YOUR FREEZER AND SLOW COOKED DESSERTS

Suet puddings are best frozen uncooked and should be thawed before slow cooking. Sponge puddings may be frozen raw or cooked. Leftover sponge pudding may be frozen and then reheated in the Slo-Cooker. Just place the pudding in an ovenproof dish, cover with foil, and pour boiling water round. Heat on Low for 1–2 hours depending on the amount being reheated.

Fruits cooked in the Slo-Cooker remain whole, so are ideally suited to freezing. Frozen fruit for pies, crumbles etc. is a great standby.

Cooked egg custards and milk puddings are not suitable for freezing. However, uncooked egg custard can be frozen; thaw before slow cooking.

CHECKPOINTS FOR SLOW COOKED DESSERTS

When adapting your own recipes for the Slo-Cooker remember:
fresh fruit will require less cooking liquid (water, wine etc.) since there is less evaporation;
dried fruit should be covered with liquid if it is to cook evenly;
pour boiling water round steamed puddings to set them off to a good start;
steamed puddings should be cooked on the High setting;
when slow cooking steamed puddings, do not fill the basin more than two thirds full—allow the pudding space to rise; it is a good idea to make a pleat in the foil or greaseproof paper covering.

Gooseberry Pie

 Serves 4

INGREDIENTS	Imperial	Metric	American
Gooseberries	12 oz.	350 g.	$\frac{3}{4}$ lb.
Sugar	2 oz.	50 g.	$\frac{1}{4}$ cup
Chopped walnuts	1 oz.	25 g.	$\frac{1}{4}$ cup
Topping :			
Self-raising flour or flour sifted with 1 tsp. baking powder	4 oz.	100 g.	1 cup
Suet, shredded or chopped	2 oz.	50 g.	$\frac{1}{3}$ cup
Caster or superfine sugar	1 oz.	25 g.	2 tbsp.
Milk	4 tbsp.	4 tbsp.	4 tbsp.
Whipped cream to decorate			
Chopped walnuts to decorate			

Pre-heat Slo-Cooker on High.

Lightly butter an ovenproof dish to just fit the
Slo-Cooker. Arrange the gooseberries in the dish and
sprinkle with the sugar and walnuts.

To make the topping, sieve the flour and stir
in the suet and sugar. Beat in the milk to make a
firm dough. Roll out the dough into a circle on a
lightly floured board to fit the dish. Lay the topping
on the gooseberries and cover the basin with buttered
foil. Stand the pudding in the Slo-Cooker and pour
round sufficient water to come half way up the sides
of the basin. Cook on High for 3–4 hours. Decorate
with whipped cream and chopped walnuts to serve.

COOKING TIME
Pre-heat while preparing ingredients.
High 3–4 hours

Almond Rhubarb Pudding

 Serves 4

INGREDIENTS	Imperial	Metric	American
Rhubarb, cut into 1 inch/2½ cm. sticks	1 lb.	450 g.	1 lb.
Sugar	3 tbsp.	3 tbsp.	3 tbsp.
Margarine	4 oz.	100 g.	½ cup
Soft brown sugar	4 oz.	100 g.	½ cup
Eggs, beaten	2	2	2
Almond essence	2 tsp.	10 ml.	2 tsp.
Self-raising flour or flour sifted with 1½ tsp. baking powder	6 oz.	175 g.	1½ cups
Cocoa powder	3 tsp.	3 tsp.	3 tsp.
Ground nutmeg	1 tsp.	1 tsp.	1 tsp.

Lightly butter the inside of Slo-Cooker and pre-heat on High. Arrange the rhubarb in the base of the Slo-Cooker and sprinkle with the sugar. In a basin, cream the margarine and sugar until light and fluffy. Gradually beat in the eggs and almond essence. Sieve together the flour, cocoa powder and nutmeg and fold in gently. Spread the mixture over the rhubarb. Cover gently with a piece of buttered greaseproof paper (butter side down). Cook on High for 3-4 hours.

COOKING TIME
Pre-heat while preparing ingredients.
High 3–4 hours

Apricot Bread and Butter Pudding

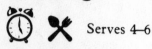 Serves 4-6

INGREDIENTS

	Imperial	Metric	American
Thin slices buttered bread	6-8	6-8	6-8
Canned apricots	14½ oz.	411 g.	medium can
Caster or superfine sugar	2 tbsp.	2 tbsp.	2 tbsp.
Eggs, beaten	3	3	3
Few drops almond essence			
Milk	¾ pt.	400 ml.	2 cups

Pre-heat Slo-Cooker on High.

Line a suitable ovenproof dish with the slices of bread (buttered side down). Drain the apricots and, reserving 5 or 6 for decoration, chop finely and scatter over the bread. Arrange any remaining bread on the fruit. Beat together the sugar, eggs and almond essence. Warm the milk to blood heat and pour onto the eggs. Pour this mixture over the bread and apricots. Cover the dish securely with buttered foil. Stand the dish in the Slo-Cooker and pour round sufficient boiling water to come half way up the sides. Cook on Low for 4-6 hours. Before serving decorate the top of the pudding with remaining apricots.

COOKING TIME
Pre-heat while preparing ingredients.
Low 4-6 hours

76

Lemon Sponge

 Serves 4

INGREDIENTS	Imperial	Metric	American
Plain flour	2 oz.	50 g.	1/4 cup
Baking Powder	1/2 tsp.	1/2 tsp.	1/2 tsp.
Cinnamon	1/2 tsp.	1/2 tsp.	1/2 tsp.
Oats, quick-cooking	2 oz.	50 g.	1/4 cup
Almonds, chopped	2 tbsp.	2 tbsp.	2 tbsp.
Butter	3 oz.	75 g.	1/3 cup
Soft brown sugar	4 oz.	100 g.	1/2 cup
Egg	1	1	1
Rind of lemon, grated	1/2	1/2	1/2
Lemon juice	1 tbsp.	1 tbsp.	1 tbsp.
Milk	1–2 tbsp.	1–2 tbsp.	1–2 tbsp.

Pre-heat Slo-Cooker on High.
Sift together the flour, baking powder and cinnamon.
Add the oats and chopped almonds. In a basin beat
together the butter and sugar until light and fluffy.
Lightly mix together the egg, lemon rind and lemon
juice and beat into the butter mixture a little at a time.
Fold in the flour along with the milk if necessary to
make a smooth dropping consistency. Put the mixture
into a buttered 1 pt./550 ml./2½ cup basin. Cover with
lightly buttered foil. Stand the basin in the Slo-Cooker
and pour round sufficient water to come half way up
the sides. Cook on High for 6–8 hours. Serve with
cream or custard.

COOKING TIME
Pre-heat while preparing ingredients.
High 6–8 hours

This pudding may also be served cold as a 'cake' iced with 3 oz./75 g./⅓ cup icing sugar mixed with 1 tbsp. lemon juice.

Baked Custard

 Serves 4

INGREDIENTS	Imperial	Metric	American
Eggs	4	4	4
Sugar, caster or superfine	2 oz.	50 g.	¼ cup
Milk	1 pt.	550 ml.	2½ cups
Few drops vanilla essence			
Grated nutmeg			

Pre-heat Slo-Cooker on High.

Blend together the eggs and sugar. Warm the milk to blood heat and pour onto the eggs. Add the vanilla essence. Pour the custard into a 1½ pt./1 litre/4 cup ovenproof dish. Sprinkle with grated nutmeg and cover with buttered foil. Stand the dish in the Slo-Cooker and pour round sufficient boiling water to come half way up its sides. Cook on Low for 5–6 hours. A knife inserted in the centre of the custard should come out clean.

COOKING TIME
Pre-heat while preparing ingredients.
Low 5–6 hours

COMPLETE MEALS

Here are some recipes specifically developed to provide a complete meal in itself. No accompaniments are needed. You can of course use many of the soup, vegetable, meat or poultry recipes in the previous sections—either as they stand or with simple, favourite additions. If your Slo-Cooker has a removable pot, try a casserole with a topping such as pastry, scone or buttered bread. They can then be crisped in the oven or under a pre-heated grill. Add dumplings to a soup or stew to make a warm and substantial meal. Simply put the dumplings in the Slo-Cooker for the final 30 minutes and cook on High setting.

Use the Slo-Cooker, too, in conjunction with other cooking equipment. Let the main course look after itself in the Slo-Cooker while you prepare an unusual or time-consuming appetiser or dessert. This is particularly handy if one course requires special last minute attention by the cook. You will find that less time is spent in the kitchen and more with your family and friends.

In the same way, a Slo-Cooker can be a boon when cooking facilities are in short supply—in a bedsitter perhaps, where there may only be one or two cooking rings. Entertaining is made considerably simpler if one course can be left to cook in the Slo-Cooker.

Experience will soon guide you as to what can be cooked and what cannot.

Finally, slow cooking is not just a British tradition. Many foreign dishes are designed for this particular method of cooking; so try preparing your favourites in your Slo-Cooker.

Paella

 Serves 6

INGREDIENTS	Imperial	Metric	American
Cooking oil	2 tbsp.	2 tbsp.	2 tbsp.
Onion, finely chopped	1	1	1
Garlic clove, crushed	1	1	1
Chicken stock	1½ pt.	900 ml.	2¾ cups
Pinch powdered saffron			
Easy-cook long grain rice	8 oz.	225 g.	1¼ cups
Tomatoes, skinned and chopped	4	4	4
Red pepper, deseeded and finely chopped	1	1	1
Cooked chicken, chopped	8 oz.	225 g.	½ lb.
Cooked mussels	6–8	6–8	6–8
Salt			
Black pepper			
Frozen peas, thawed	8 oz.	225 g.	½ lb.
Prawns	4 oz.	100 g.	¼ lb.

Pre-heat Slo-Cooker on High.

Heat the cooking oil in a large pan and saute the onion and garlic until beginning to soften. Add the chicken stock and saffron and bring to the boil. Add remaining ingredients, except peas and prawns, and bring to the boil again. Transfer to Slo-Cooker. Cook on Low for 3–4 hours. 30 minutes before serving, stir in the peas and prawns.

COOKING TIME
Pre-heat while preparing ingredients.
Low 3–4 hours

Lasagne

 Serves 6

INGREDIENTS

	Imperial	Metric	American
Lasagne	8 oz.	225 g.	½ lb.
Butter	1 oz.	25 g.	2 tbsp.
Large onion, chopped finely	1	1	1
Large clove garlic, crushed	1	1	1
Mince	1¼ lb.	550 g.	1¼ lb.
Oregano	2 tsp.	2 tsp.	2 tsp.
Salt			
Freshly ground black pepper			
Tomatoe purée or paste	4 tbsp.	4 tbsp.	4 tbsp.
Cheese sauce :			
Butter	1 oz.	25 g.	2 tbsp.
Flour	1 oz.	25 g.	¼ cup
Milk	½ pt.	300 ml.	1¼ cups
Salt and pepper			
Grated cheese	4 oz.	100 g.	¼ lb.
Parmesan cheese for topping			

Grease the inside of the Slo-Cooker and pre-heat on High. Boil the lasagne sheets in lightly salted water for 4-5 minutes to soften, then dry with kitchen paper. Heat the butter in a large pan and gently sauté the onion and garlic until transparent. Add the mince and oregano and cook for a further 3-4 minutes, stirring well. Season with salt and pepper and add the tomato purée.

To make the cheese sauce, heat the butter in a saucepan and stir in the flour. Gradually add the milk, stirring well, then bring slowly to the boil, still stirring. Season with salt and pepper and add the cheese.

Arrange a layer of mince mixture in the Slo-Cooker, followed by a layer of pasta, then cheese sauce. Continue doing this, finishing with a layer of cheese sauce. Sprinkle parmesan cheese over the top and cook on Low for 4–6 hours.

COOKING TIME
Pre-heat while preparing ingredients.
Low 4–6 hours

NOTE: If your Slo-Cooker is fitted with a removable pot the Lasagne may be browned in a hot oven or under the grill.

TO FREEZE
Leftover lasagne may be frozen in foil dishes and re-heated.
Thaw before reheating in the Slo-Cooker. To reheat: place the foil dish (covered) in the Slo-Cooker and pour round boiling water. Heat on Low (times will depend on the amount being reheated).

Chilli Con Carné

 Serves 4

INGREDIENTS

	Imperial	Metric	American
Dried red kidney beans	8 oz.	225 g.	½ lb.
Bicarbonate of soda or baking soda	1 tsp.	1 tsp.	1 tsp.
Butter	1 oz.	25 g.	2 tbsp.
Onions, chopped	2	2	2
Minced beef	1 lb.	450 g.	1 lb.
Canned tomatoes	14 oz.	397 g.	medium can
Tomato purée or tomato paste	1 tbsp.	1 tbsp.	1 tbsp.
Salt and pepper			
Chilli powder	2½ tsp.	2½ tsp.	2½ tsp.
Malt vinegar	1 tbsp.	1 tbsp.	1 tbsp.
Sugar	2 tsp.	2 tsp.	2 tsp.

Place the beans in a bowl and well cover them with water. Add the bicarbonate of soda. Leave to soak overnight.

Pre-heat Slo-Cooker on High.

Drain and rinse the beans, then boil in plenty of water for 15 minutes. Heat the butter in a large pan and sauté the onions gently until transparent. Stir in the minced beef and brown lightly. Add the remaining ingredients and bring to the boil. Transfer to Slo-Cooker. Cook on Low for 9-12 hours. Stir well before serving.

COOKING TIME
Pre-heat while preparing ingredients.
Low 9–12 hours

Chicken Risotto

 Serves 4

INGREDIENTS	Imperial	Metric	American
Cooking oil	2 tbsp.	2 tbsp.	2 tbsp.
Onions, finely chopped	2	2	2
Chicken stock	1½ pt.	900 ml.	2¾ cups
Green pepper, deseeded and finely chopped	1	1	1
Button mushrooms, chopped	4 oz.	100 g.	¼ lb.
Tomatoes, skinned and chopped	3	3	3
Easy-cook long grain rice	6 oz.	175 g.	¾ cup
Cooked chicken, chopped	8 oz.	225 g.	½ lb.
Cooked ham, chopped	2 oz.	50 g.	2 oz.

   Pre-heat Slo-Cooker on High.
Heat the cooking oil in a large pan and sauté the onions gently until beginning to soften. Add the stock and bring to the boil. Stir in remaining ingredients, bring to the boil again and transfer to Slo-Cooker. Cook on Low for 3–4 hours. Stir before serving.

COOKING TIME
Pre-heat while preparing ingredients.
Low 3–4 hours

Winter Casserole

✖ ✳ Serves 6

INGREDIENTS	Imperial	Metric	American
Cooking oil	3 tbsp.	3 tbsp.	3 tbsp.
Stewing beef, cut into cubes	2 lb.	1 kg.	2 lb.
Onions, chopped	2	2	2
Celery sticks or stalks, chopped	2	2	2
Carrots, thinly sliced	4	4	4
Large potatoes, cut into ½ in./1 cm. cubes	3	3	3
Flour	1 oz.	25 g.	2 tbsp.
Beef stock	¾ pt.	400 ml.	2 cups
Salt and pepper			
Bouquet garni			

Pre-heat Slo-Cooker on High.

Heat the cooking oil in a large pan and brown the meat lightly. Transfer to Slo-Cooker. In the same oil sauté the vegetables for about 5 minutes. Mix the flour with a little of the beef stock to form a smooth paste. Add the rest of the stock then pour over the vegetables, Add seasoning and bouquet garni. Bring to the boil then transfer to Slo-Cooker. Stir the mixture well. Cook on **High** for 30 minutes. then switch to Low for 7–10 hours.

COOKING TIME
Pre-heat while preparing ingredients.
Low 7–10 hours

TO FREEZE
Pack in rigid polythene or foil container, cover and freeze.

LITTLE EXTRAS

The recipes in this section emphasise the versatility of the Slo-Cooker. They are perhaps recipes one would not bother to prepare under normal circumstances, but because they can be prepared in the Slo-Cooker without careful attendance, are made simple and convenient.

Surprise your family with 'real' porridge for breakfast, cooked overnight in the Slo-Cooker. On more exotic lines, try heating drinks and punches to greet you late on Halloween, or after a November 5th bonfire. Christmas too is a good time to use your Slo-Cooker as a centrepiece with Spiced Wine.

Slo-Cook Gingerbread is delicious. The texture and flavour are perfect; and though the surface of the cake does not crisp and brown, the addition of a glaze gives a most attractive finish.

You will no doubt discover other uses for your Slo-Cooker. If it is kept handy on a work surface you will be tempted to use it as often as possible. Hopefully this chapter will help stimulate ideas to do just that.

Tea Punch

INGREDIENTS	Imperial	Metric	American
Tea	2 pt.	1 litre	5 cups
Red wine	1 pt.	500 ml.	2½ cups
Grated lemon rind and juice	1	1	1
Clear honey	4 tbsp.	4 tbsp.	4 tbsp.
Cinnamon stick			
Orange, sliced	1	1	1

Place all ingredients in the Slo-Cooker and heat on Low for 2 hours.

COOKING TIME
Low 2 hours

Spiced Wine

INGREDIENTS	Imperial	Metric	American
Red wine	3 pt.	1.7 litre	7½ cups
Water	¾ pt.	400 ml.	2 cups
Brandy (optional)	4 tbsp.	4 tbsp.	4 tbsp.
Rind and juice of lemon	1	1	1
Orange, sliced	1	1	1
Brown sugar	3 tbsp.	3 tbsp.	3 tbsp.
Mixed spice	1½ tsp.	1½ tsp.	1½ tsp.

Place all ingredients in the Slo-Cooker and heat on low for 2 hours.

COOKING TIME
Low 2 hours

Slo-Cook Gingerbread

 Serves 8–10

INGREDIENTS	Imperial	Metric	American
Dark soft brown sugar	8 oz.	225 g.	1 cup
Butter	6 oz.	175 g.	¾ cup
Golden syrup	12 oz.	350 g.	¾ lb.
Flour	1 lb.	450 g.	1 lb.
Salt	1 tsp.	1 tsp.	1 tsp.
Ground ginger	3–4 tsp.	3–4 tsp.	3–4 tsp.
Baking powder	2 tsp.	2 tsp.	2 tsp.
Egg	1	1	1
Milk	½ pt.	300 ml.	1¼ cups
Chopped peel and cherries, mixed	1 tbsp.	1 tbsp.	1 tbsp.
To glaze:			
Sugar	2 oz.	50 g.	4 tbsp.
Water	2 tbsp.	2 tbsp.	2 tbsp.

Pre-heat Slo-Cooker on High.
Lightly butter a 7 in./15 cm. round cake tin
(preferably non-stick). In a saucepan, melt the sugar,
butter and syrup gently until the sugar is dissolved.
Allow to cool. Sieve the dry ingredients into a basin,
make a well in the centre and pour in the melted
mixture, egg and milk. Stir well to form a smooth
consistency. Pour the mixture into the prepared tin
and sprinkle the chopped peel and cherries over the
top. Cover with buttered foil and stand the tin in the
Slo-Cooker. Pour round sufficient boiling water to
come half way up the sides of the tin. Cook on High
for 6–8 hours. Turn the gingerbread out of the tin.
Blend together the sugar and water and brush it over
the top of the gingerbread immediately. Allow to cool.

COOKING TIME
Pre-heat while preparing ingredients.
High 6–8 hours

TO FREEZE
Interleave slices of gingerbread with greaseproof paper and wrap securely in foil. This way, individual servings may be taken from the freezer.

CHECKPOINT
Invert a small, ovenproof container in the Slo-Cooker, to lift the tin clear of the base and to assist its easy removal.

Porridge

 Serves 4

INGREDIENTS	Imperial	Metric	American
Water	$1\frac{1}{2}$ pt.	900 ml.	$3\frac{3}{4}$ cups
Oatmeal	4 oz.	100 g.	$\frac{1}{4}$ lb.
Salt	$\frac{1}{2}$ tsp.	$\frac{1}{2}$ tsp.	$\frac{1}{2}$ tsp.

Boil the water in a saucepan and sprinkle the oatmeal over, stirring continuously. Add the salt then transfer to Slo-Cooker. Cook on Low for about 8 hours or overnight.

COOKING TIME
Pre-heat while preparing ingredients.
Low 8 hours.

WEIGHTS AND MEASURES

Ingredients used in the recipes to follow are given in Imperial, Metric and American measures. Generally speaking the Metric and American measures are not exact equivalents of their Imperial counterparts. I find it better to work in quantities which have been rounded off to convenient measures. Where I have felt it important to be accurate, exact equivalents are given. It is wise to follow one set of measures; do not skip from one set to another.

All spoon and cup measures are level unless otherwise stated.

The Imperial pint measures 20 fluid ounces; the American pint measures 16 fluid ounces.

When cans of food are included in a recipe, the weights given on the label are quoted—these are usually exact equivalents.

When converting your own recipes from Imperial to Metric, or vice versa, use the tables below as guidelines.

CAPACITY

Imperial	Metric
$\frac{1}{4}$ pt. (5 fl. oz.)	150 ml.
$\frac{1}{2}$ pt. (10 fl. oz.)	300 ml.
$\frac{3}{4}$ pt. (15 fl. oz.)	400 ml.
1 pt. (20 fl. oz.)	500–600 ml.
$1\frac{1}{2}$ pt.	900 ml.
$1\frac{3}{4}$ pt.	1 litre
2 pt.	1.1 litre

SPOON CAPACITY

1 level teaspoonful = 5 millilitres or 1 × 5 ml.
spoonful.
2 level teaspoonsful = 10 ml. or 2 × 5 ml. sp.
1 level tablespoonful = 15 ml. or 1 × 15 ml. sp.

WEIGHT

Imperial	Metric
1 oz.	25 g.
2 oz.	50 g.
3 oz.	75 g.
4 oz.	100–125 g.
5 oz.	150 g.
6 oz.	175 g.
8 oz.	225 g.
10 oz.	275 g.
12 oz.	350 g.
14 oz.	400 g.
16 oz. (1 lb.)	450 g.
1½ lb.	700 g.
2 lb.	900 g. (1000 g. = 1 kg.)
3 lb.	1.4 kilograms (kg.)

INDEX

96